THE BANQUET

Stav Poleg's debut poetry collection, *The City* (Carcanet, 2022) was chosen for the *Financial Times'* Best Summer Books 2022, and was shortlisted for the Seamus Heaney Poetry Prize for First Collection, 2023. Her poetry has appeared on both sides of the Atlantic, in *The New Yorker*, *Kenyon Review*, *Poetry Daily*, *Poetry London*, *Poetry Ireland Review*, *PN Review* and elsewhere. A selection of her work is featured in *New Poetries VIII* (Carcanet, 2021). Her graphic-novel installation, 'Dear Penelope: Variations on an August Morning', created with artist Laura Gressani, was acquired by the Scottish National Gallery of Modern Art. Her theatre work was read at the Traverse Theatre, Edinburgh, and the Shunt Vaults, London, and most recently at Kettle's Yard gallery, Cambridge. She serves on the editorial board of *Magma Poetry* magazine and teaches for the Poetry School on a range of subjects including poetry inspired by the *Divine Comedy*, the *Odyssey* and the cinema of Fellini. She lives in Cambridge, UK.

THE
BANQUET
STAV POLEG

CARCANET POETRY

First published in Great Britain in 2025 by
Carcanet
Main Library, The University of Manchester
Oxford Road, Manchester, M13 9PP
www.carcanet.co.uk

A CIP catalogue record for this book is
available from the British Library.

ISBN 978 1 80017 511 2

Book design by Andrew Latimer, Carcanet
Typesetting by LiteBook Prepress Services
Printed in Great Britain by SRP Ltd, Exeter, Devon

MIX
Paper | Supporting
responsible forestry
FSC
www.fsc.org   FSC® C014540

The publisher acknowledges financial
assistance from Arts Council England.

Supported using public funding by
ARTS COUNCIL
ENGLAND

CONTENTS

THE CITADEL OF THE MIND
  The Letter   13
  Field Study   17
  Memory and Geography   20
  The Citadel of the Mind   23
  Absolute Scenes   32
  A Wandering   36

AUTUMN
  Meaning Something is like Going
    Towards Someone   41
  Autumn   44
  Nocturne   48
  The Banquet   50
  Self-Portrait as Autumn Fields   64
  Snow Leopard and Dark-Iris Lakes   66
  The Pain or the Piano-Tuning   72

UN AMOUR DÉSESPÉRÉ
  All Haulers   79
  Un Amour Désespéré   87
  Une Gaîté Divine   88
  Le Malheur a été Mon Dieu   89
  Film   95
  Affogato   98
  Love, an Accident in a Substance   100
  Playing Fields   114

Notes   121
Acknowledgements   123

For my children

…you have found a new conception. As if you had invented a new way of painting; or, again, a new metre, or a new kind of song.

—Wittgenstein, *Philosophical Investigations,* §401

THE CITADEL OF THE MIND

THE LETTER

Think of it as an installation—
on a glass table, a ceramic-blue
plate—an invitation—

margarita on ice, a hand reaching
for an orange segment, perhaps
it is summer, the changing

of weather. Perhaps you've just
got off the train. The sky like a boy playing
with sunset—you don't know

how it happened, you don't have to
explain. The street is a sunflower
field. The sea, an ongoing

question. Some things
are like this—the traffic, the trees—
an aesthetic dispute—an oscillation—

and far off—the forest
of uneven streets—a karaoke bar
pulsing heat and night

weather. How the light
takes hold of the traffic, the river's dark
floor. How the dark travels

upwards—the coal-silver stars
like a far-off vacation, the inconsistency
of a moon crescent—you know

how it works—it's midsummer, the distance
of stars moving further, the rain
coming in

like a fine stage-direction. Think of it
as a study in pain against
language—the river, the trees—

there's always a thought moving
closer, an unscheduled thunder, a storm
in a picture you're still holding

close. I have to admit—I didn't expect
to see you this early, carrying
a letter—the same one

you tore into pieces years and countries
ago. I think what happened
is this—

you must have managed
to go back in time. Time? Think of it
as a provocation—

a yellow leaf caught in blue-bicycle
weather, a train testing distance
with an inaccurate

question, an equation of words against
speed. It's been raining all day but look—
you have managed to draw your way

here. There are so many windows
in the towering building over the bridge
but only one window

is lit with waves of blue and dark
green. Think of it as a repetition—
on the seventh floor

a woman is watching the same film
she's never able to watch. Some things
are too close, and how often

they move even closer
in films. But this evening, as the rain
plays with darkness across the landscape

of streets, she's leaning against
the half-open window, running a thought
at full speed. The moon—

a recurring wrong
question. The street, a loose
string. Perhaps you've been running for days

in this weather. Perhaps you've just
got off the train. And yes,
there was never

a letter, only a chamber—the movement
of words against words. You don't have
to explain. Some letters

open and close
like an unwritten rumour
but they matter, they matter. How else

would you walk in this wide field
of thought—the moon as the trace
of a hot-air balloon, the night—a train

station. You don't know
how it happens. You don't know
how it happens.

FIELD STUDY

That year, I wanted to know
everything—the word and the matter, the sky

taking off at the edge of the sea, the bell
ringing and ringing in a locked-summer

castle, the city aching
under the burden

of snow—the moon carried
by water like an unsettled

vow—knowing the direction
would not grant protection—I knew

that—I wanted to know
the night gathering speed like a heightened

emotion, the kingfisher
river, the blue-scaffolding forest

leading towards the streets wrestling
with warmth—knowing

the city would not clear my pain—I knew
that—I wanted to know

the smoke and the rainstorm, the girl
on the opposite balcony—

the way she was studying
a tangerine segment

under the ringing-blue light
of a brass microscope—I wanted to study

the air when it rained and just after
it settled, the room opened to light, all

the ways to say *heart* without
meaning *mind*, the harbour

testing out waves and new water, the moon
turning into a fictional landscape—all

year I think I was trying
to write you a letter—something

to do with the city holding onto the night
like a call for attention,

something to do with the premise
of youth as aesthetic escape or a visual

contract—I liked that, I'm not sure
I knew what it meant—perhaps

that I kept losing things—not ideas
but things—real, absolute things—those

that mattered—the rain
in a picture I was trying to hold, the distance

it took for a call to reach
somewhere. The smoke as a shield

against warmth. All year
I was sick—sick of knowing

so little. Sick of longing. Knowing
the direction would not bring

you back—there was nothing I didn't know
about that, and I had to know

everything—everything
else—there was so little to lose

when the city offered that much
to learn—how I wanted

to believe in that—
how I wished I could trust my whole

heart in the high castles of dark—
in the great, volatile cities of knowledge.

There's a point at the edge of the field
in a book I'm reading where a river I thought was missing
turns into a film: a case of absence flowering

action—a yellow bicycle on a metallic-blue bridge—
something like this—a bluish pink feather, the unsettled
green in a silver-dark sea, and in a different

country, I mean—chapter, the irregularity
of autumn fields, the beauty of snow or of things
when repeated. Maybe there's an algorithm

creating a sunset—each page, a split-second
later, a lake getting fuller and fuller, a room I'm trying
to fit myself in. Surely there's an argument

to be made against sunsets—how inadequate
they are, how assured and self-indulgent—a recurring
intervention in the memory of streets. Consider the rain

as two opposite lands—two possible soundtracks
for a sleepless, long week—the principle
of uncertainty—the certitude of clarity—something

in between. Outside, the city is rising in circular
movement like a fast-flying machine. You see, here's a thing
I never understand—it's only when I'm running

that time seems to happen at the right pace. Could you
help with that? The city is moving—the river, the buildings,
cyclists, junctions, newspapers, lampposts, some

bridges, train stations, trees. Today, for example,
it's snowing—a film crew is shooting a scene
at the end of the street. It must be the seaside, midsummer—

a girl with heavy sunglasses holding onto a blue parasol
as if it were a quick helium balloon. On the news, a storm
is given a name—the sea is hysterical, the sky pulsing

cerulean and pink like a feast. I know what you'd say—
we're part of this scenery, no matter how irrational
the weather is. There's so much noise but the music

is real. There are so many songs. How beautiful
the sky tonight, how frightening and real—we could almost
turn it into a film. The past as a mathematical object—

would you agree? A system of clear
borders, patterns and doors that keep sliding forwards
and backwards towards the long list of credits and names

at the end of a film—the edge of a field
in a book I'm reading where a river I thought missing
turns into a bicycle wheel, a yellow feather, a scene in the snow

in the height of summer just when the camera
moves in. Somewhere, a girl wrestles with an upturned
umbrella as if it were a rebelling idea or the unstable heart

of an open-air thought. Somewhere it's always
snowing and always midsummer. I don't know
how it works. The sunsets go backwards and forwards

like unsettled clocks. As for the irregularity
of buildings, streets, rivers—as for the nights burning
their full-hearted bridges—how they glow and withdraw

into the next movement of words—maybe there's an algorithm
that could measure the distance between absence
and action—the precarious point

when the night turns into a spiralling road—the moon
beaming disorder like a heady cocktail, the news
naming more stories, more cities and storms, and far off—

on an unlikely cliff or a snowy mountain overlooking
the nest of a silver-moon lake—the city, protective
and real—an exaltation of words. Is this how a story

begins—with the inconclusiveness of loss? There's a country
I took for a landscape I wanted to restructure and change, at least
in a film—a story I wanted to breathe

from the start, call it memory, call it geography, call it
the vast landscape of childhood or night—a thing
disappearing—a country turning into a map.

THE CITADEL OF THE MIND

First you were an idea, a blue satellite
orbiting a distant, dark

moon. Then you were a feather, the light
distance it takes for beauty

to form into something like finding
the ground. It didn't happen

without warning, the morning
glowed like a feverish neon sign—an indication

of clemency—I thought, the sky
turned sapphire and dark like new foreign

fire—a transposition
from fear to loss—how wrong

I was. How wrong
was the weather, raining and raining

without pause. I've always thought
there was one primary source—

not light or fire but the small
movement from sound

into a word. The leaping fish
was glowing from blue to bright turquoise

when moving upstream
or was it a song I was trying

to catch—a foreign soundscape
floating above the wide-open highway

when heading back home? First
you were an idea. Then, an idea

with wings—the purpose of flying
or shifting the weight between travel

and dream. Today, I'm reading
that *the Vita Nuova tells of dream visions*

and feverish hallucinations. It's late
afternoon, the shortest

day of the year. There are so many ways
to lock oneself out of a castle, out of a word

that threatens to destabilise
a sentence, a faraway kingdom, the heart

of a scene. Love
and the trembling of light when it reaches

the water. Love like a highway—a misapprehension
of speed. First you were stretching

your arms, testing the wingspan of grief—
it was not theoretical—you've known

for too long how it feels. Knowledge
and grief—the strange forces

of water when they reach a new land—
no—it's not that. Knowledge

and grief—a theatre scene carrying
the weight of an unpronounced

word—no, not *quite* what I mean. First
you turned loss into a symbol, a primary

myth. Then you found dreaming—the sounds
taking flight in a faraway

street. That you carried a sign like a country—
that you weren't able to let go—

was that grief? The empiricist
insists on realism, dreams

may come later, dreams are the function
of a visual mind. Dreams are echoes

and interpretations. There's order, sure—
there's order even in chaos

theory—patterns, equations, the long
calculations of matter as time. The historian

considers primary sources as if they were numbers
not words. The poet is a pragmatist—making

something out of the strange promise
of nothing—words

are important but not *that*
important. First you were an idea, then

a dark river, an arrow, a field fractured
with lights. The philosopher seeks

the truth. Truth, the poet thinks, how unusual
and noble, how responsible

and full of trust. The poet is a pragmatist—
she prefers to play. Play, like sleep or love

is the most serious thing—the poet
claims. Sure—the physicist

says before heading towards the river
that cuts through opposite

notions of time—whatever you say.
In the *Convivio*, in the battle of knowledge

versus love—Lady Philosophy
wins, hands down. But Dante tells us

that Beatrice is still there, still walking
around, still *holding the citadel of my mind*—

the citadel of the mind—
like a chamber of flashing blue light—

is struck with new fire, lightning, the fierce
temper of rain. Time

has passed but the mind
does not do time. The mind refuses

time as a gift made of distance
and light. The physicist understands

time in relation to space
and gravity—time is the fourth dimension

in a physical non-metaphorical
sense: there is no such thing as Space

but Space-Time. The heart, the heart
is constructed of four chambers, the poet

tries. The poet studies time like a theatre
scene—the fourth wall

like a curtain of time between language
and play. On the stage, time

can be anything—a theatre
prop: an hourglass full of running blue

sand. The actor takes the small
hourglass before tossing it towards the ceiling

again and again. Time, like a target
moving, time like a dark implication, a realization

of heat. The actor picks up
the broken, uneven

fragments of glass from the sand-covered
floor. The poet goes out of the theatre, takes

the first bus and starts running, running
in words. Reading physics is like drinking

ten cups of espresso in one
hour—the poet contemplates—my mind

is high on physics—my heart
is flying on so much caffeine. Time—

like a want or a miscalculation—
is that it? In the *Convivio*, letting

Beatrice go is turning her into a leading
idea—the sketch of a castle

before building a castle. Does it work? Well,
in the *Purgatorio*, Beatrice will come back

less as an idea, more as an undefeatable
force. First you were a satellite, then

a dark forest, a fortress of words. You turned love
into knowledge, darkness into a wrestling

ring—the audacity of language
when it gathers more speed. Yes, I know—

I must accept—not everything
is about loss. Not all philosophy

was forced to be written out of exile, the deep
soundscape or grief. Not every word

was invented due to the loss of another—
O.K., sure, but most did. The poet is circling

and circling a word like a feverish
hawk—time—a dark arrow

with wings, no, it's not that. Time, an invisible
wall between language and play. Well—

time—like love or sleep, destabilising
a scene—no, still not quite

what I'm trying to say. Time, like losing
someone, losing brilliantly, exceptionally, losing

mathematically, theatrically, losing with all
chambers of hearts—and not losing

them at all, not losing one bit—is that
right? There's this thing Einstein wrote

in the letter to the sister of his best friend:
Now he has departed from this strange world

a little ahead of me. That signifies
nothing. For those of us who believe

in physics, the distinction
between past, present and future is only

a stubbornly persistent illusion. Yes, the poet
says, count me in—I'm a believer

in physics—that's what I meant
when I said *play*. First

you were an idea—a flying formation
of words, then an admission—

time—no, I do not understand
how it works. The poet is a pragmatist—

in *Paradiso* 30, Beatrice will give Dante
a departing message full of sadness and play—

luce intellettüal, piena d'amore—
maybe that's why it was always about

the citadel of the mind
not the chambers of heart. The mind—

the mind has to work so much harder
when confronted

with loss. The mind must be pragmatic—
construct a fortress, lose

itself in theatre, physics—anything—
to accommodate the heart's erratic

notes. First you were an idea, then an idea
with wings—it didn't

work. Then you became a citadel, a strange
castle to walk around or throw

your heart in. The heart
has four chambers, the poet

thinks—why is that so exciting? Like the four
dimensions, the four directions, the fourth

trembling wall. The poet
is a moralist—how on earth

has this happened? Well, words
are important but not *that*

important—the poet believes in the material
reality of right and wrong. First

you were an idea—a gift
of belonging, the distance it takes

to fall into form—but then something
happened, something

so dark you were not able to utter or carry
with words. A moralist,

the poet will come to the conclusion
that knowledge has little to do with ethics

and everything to do
with loss. Grief, like a city expanding, grief

like the four highways
of a heart. The mind is fearless—

it will do anything—build
a citadel, move stars

across a map, construct new forests of lights
and dark rivers, the mathematics

of space and time—whatever it takes
to carry what's left from one's language

or childhood, whatever it takes to carry what's left
from the heart.

ABSOLUTE SCENES

>After Dante, *Purgatorio*
>...*non sapei tu che qui è l'uom felice?*

London, spring equinox. There are absolute scenes
in the airport leading towards this dream. The ceiling is tilting,
turning into the floor. It's snowing in here so I'm pressing
the skylight into the blue-icy fog and look—in the distance—
a ship trying the sapphire-green sea like an incomplete
thought—beautiful—a star forms in the dark like a small provocation,
and three more! The sky, an unsettled machine. Look, I'm now deep
in season two of *A Kind of Middle Point.* Can we call it that? A kind
of middle point—time according to Aristotle (Physics) or the point
between deficiency and excess (Ethics) and, yes—what the hell
is going on? So many questions—the girl driving a car
in the rain instead of a poem, is she heading towards or leaving
the cliffs hanging over the sea? May I say how I love
the title song: *England, an Invitation.*

England, an invitation in the form of a lingua-franca
machine, a strong sense of failure and as good a place as any
for "What are writers for?" Dear reader, pick up a stick, circle
the false answer: for climbing steep, spherical
islands / turning words into photosensitive films / playing
poets *and* the main characters / trying out physics
and ethics / getting lost in the middle of things / taking dreams
literally, trains symbolically / misreading subject for matter, choice
for free-will. Here in the city of reconfiguration, let me
offer you a map as a question, an island as a mountain
and a lost-property dream. Now, as the hour of sea-surfers
carries longing like prayer—a recurring
short film—dear dreamer, fasten your seatbelt
as we gear up for language, I mean landing, I mean, I mean,

Language, I mean landing, I mean, I mean—
all day on the train to King's Cross I'm running in Dante
towards the gate, the two flickering locks, the precarious point
where Purgatorio begins. Dear runner, my fellow newcomer—
how is time working for you? How is longing? Years of practice
and I'm still failing in both. So instead, I'll be trying
to draw characters into this land, I mean story, the way a thought
could lift the shadow of Ulysses from the eighth circle
of Hell to the siren catching his name on this steep-terrace
walk. Here, on the cliff of show-off and hunger, here
on the Circle Line platform towards Liverpool Street, take the keys
to that thing you have split into unequal halves and named
talent and discipline—dear runner, you who are always
a newcomer in another wild scene—open the gates.

In another wild scene—open the gates. London,
send your ships and fast-flying machines, take me to the shores
of Tate Modern's turbine hall and concrete pyramid and a 'Fellini
Celebration' at the BFI—yay! (There are so many staircases
in *La Dolce Vita*, so many spirals, exits, uprooted sculptors
and ceilings, ruined and locked doors.) Remember, reader, the river
caught in the night like a question, the Northern Line pulsing
new fog, the girl climbing up the down escalator, eager to miss
the train home—her bag falling, keys, books, her phone heading
towards the floor? Midway upon running in Dante I have reached
the Terrace of Wrath. Here in the land of overground circles
and high-altitude cranes, here where a thought is as solid and real
as the matter that wrestles with it until it takes form—*And you
have a mind that planets cannot rule and stars concern.*

A mind that planets cannot rule and stars concern—a thing so
real it turns matter to more matter, more stairways and bridges, more
air. And you have a city you're trying to rein—an image, a word—
shall we go over the plan? The night as a vacant cathedral / train
station? Yes. The fully conceived Negroni Sbagliato? Ma certo!
Getting lost on the terrace of wrath? Dear reader, I'm here, running
in Dante all night at King's Cross. And what about time, matter,
space? I'm thinking of Peter Brook's, *with a cut the mind
can flick from yesterday to Australia*—here in the city
of theatre makers, shall we go into that? As for vice versus
sin—vice as the Aristotelian take—a tendency for wrongdoing
rather than definite, absolute sin—a different kind of losing
direction—higher and deeper and so full of change—dear Dante—
dear poet and protagonist—plug this into my vein.

Plug this into my vein: the river, the fire, the three
poets climbing towards a towering forest—a different
kind of losing direction, the clearest-blue air. As for hunger
and why the shades in this place still experience
it—as for pain—since climbing this rock has always involved
some kind of prayer, poetry, unsettled scripts, I'll be going for
Wittgenstein: *You learned the concept 'pain' in learning
language.* You learned the concept 'absence' by uttering
a name. Three times Virgil is called—three times
he drifts further away. Here, where your own loss is part
of an always much greater anarchy, here where the night carries
sunsets and dawns like recurring-dark questions:
*How were you able to ascend the mountain? Did you not know
that man is happy here?* England, an invitation.

England, an invitation—a different kind of losing
direction—bigger and far greater on the unruly threshold
of season three. Dear runner, if you struggle to handle the angels
wielding seven candelabras, the air—blue with cold fire, the four
creatures each with six wings, or those wild, wild visions
of the apocalypse, remember this—you may drive down
in circles all the way back to the terrace of wrath—a kind
of middle point. I'll be here, back in canto sixteen, studying
the wounds that can burn in the dark across language and
matter, I mean—time. Longing, hunger, the velocity
of loss—*you who are free are subject*—at what point
does a city turn into one's own subject and matter, the language
you carry and care for, the streets you're running and trying
to dream? London, spring equinox, there are absolute scenes.

A WANDERING

La scrittura è stella piena di luce
—Dante, *Convivio*

The author holds onto a word like testing the rupture
of sound—something like light breaking out
of a disquieted star. A wandering. *The soul reveals itself*

in the mouth almost like colour
behind glass. Maybe some books are not meant
to be put aside, maybe once opened—they've broken

something within the reader—the one holding
the words close in her palms. A deep, singular cut
emitting sharp light, a heightened pain, a road ascending

towards the fracture of night—the closest one's been
to an understanding—something like this: a point
of respite. I'm back to Dante, studying

the fissure and impulse of sound—*And what is laughter*
if not a coruscation of the soul's delight, a light
appearing outside in accordance

with what is within? Authority: the declaration
of an author—*atto d'autore*—an action of writing, a word
taking shape like a wave of attention, a wandering

sound. There are two words in Italian
for *knowing*—two words chasing each other, moving
apart—*Sapere*: to know. *Conoscere*: to know, know

deeply, to know someone, to recognise, I think
there's something here to do with longing—an action
of running backward and forward, a wave breaking

out of a disquieted star. *True study*—Dante says—
is the *application of the mind to the thing
it is in love with.* The author looks after a word

until it grows into a creature of flight. The application
of the mind. The thing it is in love with. Some books,
once soaring out of the window and into the night

will not be restrained, will not be brought back
to the ground. In Latin, *Studium* has two meaning—
two rebelling minds: *study*, sure, but also—

excitement—enthusiasm. *La scrittura è stella
piena di luce*—*Writing is a star full of light.* A star full
of fracture. The author carries a word like a chest

heavy with flight. The reader enters the room
of a book, holding onto the night as if it were made
of dark, wandering letters. An application. A sort of attention

to sound. *A star full of light which manifests the field
of knowledge.* A wave of delight. You are one thing, reader,
and then you're another. A holder of light.

AUTUMN

MEANING SOMETHING IS LIKE GOING TOWARDS SOMEONE

After Wittgenstein, *Philosophical Investigations*,
§455 and §457

In the story, a metropolis took off like a dark-flying
machine—a ship floating on air—the bridges opened
and stretched, letting go of the river, waving
silver-dark wings. In the story, a stone
fell from the sky like a closing-in
fear—leaving a hole on the path heading
towards the sea. There's a note
I've been drawing and throwing away
like an unsettled sketch—in a different country
a girl is always still running, crossing
a field. The moon as a newly formed
question, the road testing out
directions—there are always new stories
to leave or begin. It's been snowing all morning
in the city I'm missing, in the moon-chasing
streets of a faraway
thought. It's been raining all night so I'm trying
to draw. There's a train travelling backwards
in a black-and-white scene. There's a hell of a party
on the warm-solstice shore I'm quite eager
to miss. Some dreams
are like this. On the bus I'm reading
that a field in physics is a region where each point
is affected by a force. There's a neon-blue siren
crossing our street like a deepening
cut, there's the blue

of a leaf in the flowering snow. In the poetry
class I ask the students to test home as the country
of memory. There's always a street leading into
another, a train leaving a station, an unwritten
letter, a girl carrying a word
like a flamed-metal sword. In the improvised
darkness we watch *I Vitelloni* and note how Fellini
reconstructed his hometown of Rimini
in Ostia, Rome. I can't understand
why this evening keeps stretching its wings
like a mounting sub-plot—why it's never difficult
to reimagine the sea: to add movement, a disquieting
storm, why home and imprecision
go together disproportionately well, why a poem
is a small probability that forms and
reforms. There's a train in the story I tend
to forget but it keeps coming back—unannounced—
like a quote—*We go towards the thing*
we mean. In the story there are children and an airplane
racing towards the shore, a girl crossing the field
of an evening, as street after street draws away
and takes off. Dear reader, here are the gates
to the city I hold onto, hold
onto and never let go. Here is the road leading
towards the door I'm still trying
to draw. There's a point
in the distance and I think you are there—moving
further away as I'm driving to tell you the thing
I keep whispering and saying out loud—like a code
or an unwritten note—so I won't forget
how to say it, or whether I left it
back there—in the forest of incomplete
bridges and rivers and dark-silver

smoke, as the night—like all readers
in streetlights and snow—lifts its wings
before changing direction, soaring and leaving
the seashore, the story, the city I'm still running towards
and from.

AUTUMN

This morning, the city is floating
under a metal-blue moon. The streets holding

their lights—rain-fractured and high—
like open-night

scars. There is so much autumn
in this shattered-heart

evening. In the distance—a field taking off
in the blue-fire dark. All week

you are curled on the sofa
in pain—the light throbs on your skin

like cut glass. There are so many
ways to leave a door open. So many ways

to pick up the phone
without falling apart. In the picture

I'm trying to find all night
there's an upside-down bicycle and a child

running after a cat. I don't know
where I left it. This morning, the city

is shaking—a dark, volatile
star. The heart is a floating-map

chamber—I write
on the train—so I don't forget, so I know

how to find it—
the heart is a harbour, the deep structure

of night.
Somewhere, a blue horse

stretches its wings above purple-blue
rivers and light carrying

lakes. Somewhere, a heart
is thrown like a disk

on the cold metal field. I once woke up
in a different country and it was still

out of reach. The moon you drew
in your childhood is the moon you're failing

to capture tonight in this faraway
country—in this rain flowering

street. I once walked in the rain all year
and the moon turned

into a shield. This morning, you're curled
on the sofa in pain. Childhood

returned like a tidal wave ready to soar
in the instant of dark—an old, structural

fear. There are so many
ways to leave a door locked and

fist-broken. So many ways
to grieve. All week you're not crying

on the bus, not crying on the train, not crying
at work. All week you're the only

one in this cold autumnal city
not talking of your childhood

home. This morning the city is floating
in sharp luminous haze—a ship

heading towards the absence of water, the deep
aching of night. I once heard

that the name of the place
you grew up in becomes a synonym

for *childhood*—two words
indistinguishable—

like *nightfall* and *dream*. Like *longing*
and *running*. Two words carrying

each other—like *leaving*
and *writing*. Two words stretching

their wings. This autumn—
the city—my city—I'm not sure

what it is—I once woke up
in my new country and the moon vanished

into a metal-blue ring. There are so many
ways to leave a door shaken. So many ways

to leave. Last night you tripped over
the upside-down bicycle, the child

running, the cat. How to hold onto a picture
and never let go. Keep

trying. How to sit on the train
and stop crying—this, once it's started—this

I don't know. I once heard
that your most formative years

will take shape from the age of zero
to five. How curious is that. How

shattering. A small, quiet word
will form in the delicate map

of your mind—like the endless night sky
of the desert, the warm nightfall

of autumn, the small
heartbeats of stars, the love

and the sorrow, the mind and the heart
of the mind—a word

that means only one thing—*childhood, childhood*—
and this is mine—Be'eri— בְּאֵרִי —

NOCTURNE

This evening, the city carries the sky
like a chamber of rain. In the distance, a ship
taking over a coastline I'm trying

to draw before it draws back. Here,
the street is moon sapphire—a purposeful
light—nightfall before nightfall

takes over the harbour's deep shadow
of water and flight. The blue is never dark blue
unless you fall into the widening

sky of a city breaking apart—a character
said in the book I wanted
to give you. The stars moving

over a field—all the things
I wanted to give you. This evening, the river
forms into a screen—to take in

the city and streetlights, the full movement
of night—a map of the dark. You know
what I love? I love air pollution

in film. The silver-blue lightning
of smoke and dark hearts. The anguish
of rain. How to breathe in

a city that's moving away. How to leave
and keep coming back. A forest of rain
in a penultimate scene is something

I get—rain as a lead-in—rain as the heart
of more rain. A blue note in the snow
as a sign of escape—an autumnal-blue

light in a streetcorner café—I remember
that place. I remember the city mistaken
for film like a study in smoke against

glass—the moon like a target of light
in the dark—I remember that place, that
moment, where everything stops and belongs

to the night—each sunset and streetlight, each
sigh, all the things I wanted to give you—
the moon and the river, the wide chamber of sky.

THE BANQUET

... per lo naturale amore della propia loquela
—Dante, *Convivio*

It was a difficult autumn, I reached for Dante
because I needed to walk out, needed to be taken

by the dark, unreliable highway
that links ethics to knowledge. All winter

I found myself running in the spiralling evenings
and streets of Florence—a city haunted

by longing—a road leading inwards
and outwards—shaken

with grief. The *Convivio*—a love
letter to philosophy, a memoir, a study

in banishment—I'm still trying
to pin down what it is—was composed

in vernacular Florentine—away
from Florence—in exile—somewhere

between 1304 and 1307. Time, like theatre,
is a matter of action taking on

space—a foreign-night landscape
turning into the sound of a footstep, an imminent

threat. A city cannot be carried
from one place to another—but words

can be lifted with ease. Anger, too,
is lighter than joy—lighter than pleasure—

is so easy to carry—anger is the most
reliable matter—it won't

break—does not need to be looked
after. Anger—like language—

will survive exile *and* earthquake. Florence,
a city haunted by heartache, will take off

in the form of words whispered
around family meals, words tossed before

bedtime, words hovering under skies fascinated
by stars hiding from thunder, words

shaken at midnight before dreams reach
their own visual take on absence

and hunger—it was a difficult spring, a very
difficult summer. I reached for Dante

because I needed to be taken, needed
to breathe. The *Convivio*, the Banquet, a feast

reconstructing a city out of intimate rumours
and weeping, desolate streets—I think we can call it

a study in language, or longing, or language
as longing—I'm still trying to figure it out.

*

Dante dived into Aristotle—*il mio maestro*—
in Latin—years before Aristotle's work

was discovered in Greek. Aristotle—
who *wrote on nearly every subject*

imaginable—according to the dual-language
Critical Edition I'm trying

to read to the sound of thunder wrestling
with speed all the way on the bus

towards King's Cross. Aristotle hovers
over Dante's Florence like the God

of earthly knowledge—words
will lead you towards more

knowledge, words will move you
towards the good. Three quarters

of Aristotle's works—on Prayer, on Justice,
on Comedy—among others—

were lost. Dante's *Convivio*—
a banquet designed to serve fifteen meals

of poetry and prose in everyday language—
was never completed—a project

on language that, like language, breaks
into every subject *imaginable*—

astronomy, logic, equality, love, maths,
rhetoric, Latin, hunger, hypocrisy, and of course—

heartbreak. Florence, a city haunted
by soaring ambition and moral

corruption—Florence—a city fractured
by a hundred towers testing out

storms—Florence—a city disfigured
by a singular, unbearable

loss—will hold onto language and take flight
like a hawk circling the point of true

source—a matter of hunger—a sort
of absence—words

will take on hunger *and* absence, breathe
them into a force. It was a difficult

summer, I held onto Dante like to a critical
thought. That day on the bus, the storm

took over the city like a desperate
flight. A study in fear. There was something

I found heartbreaking, even though
I knew it was not meant to be—

the *Convivio* is written *out of natural love*
for my own language—

...per lo naturale amore della propia loquela.

Everything you learned, you first learned
with your first words—everything—even

heartbreak, even silence, even
another language.

                    *

*All human beings by nature desire
to know*—the first book of the *Convivio*

begins—a quote from Aristotle—a prayer
for ethics to pull itself together, to seek

knowledge with words. *It's wanting to know
that makes us matter*—the closed, difficult

character in Tom Stoppard's *Arcadia*
will say on stage before opening her book, leaving

towards her notes. I remember the light going off
at the theatre space—I was still new

in London—London was still a city of insecure
words—the rain took hold of the streets

like an irregular prayer—each house, a study
in rain, each word, a sigh

made of rain. Each letter, each
thunder—a summer of rain. I was trying

to find my father but he wouldn't
respond. The city took me

without notice—an open, indifferent
landscape—the most difficult and most

welcoming, I was trying to learn
how it worked. That summer, I was no longer

an outsider but an official
outsider—a foreigner

in a city haunted by words. *It's wanting to know
that makes us matter.* I remember

carrying these words like a sigh
or a prayer, perhaps a way of coping

with something—back then
I didn't want to believe

in loss—*it's wanting to know
that makes us matter—it's wanting to know—*

*

A city cannot be carried from one place
to another, but thoughts can be lost

and recovered in seconds—the weight
of a sound flowing into a chamber, a wave

forming into a word. Wittgenstein
wrote the *Philosophical Investigations*

in German—away from the German
language—in Cambridge, England—away

from what happened between 1929
and 1947—a project on language

written to the constant new soundscape
of foreign words—a way of pushing

towards some order, a wave flowing into
another, perhaps a desire for linear thought—

After several unsuccessful attempts
to weld my results together into such a whole,

I realized that I should never succeed.
What never succeeded, collapsed

into a wild, beautiful landscape—
a work I will always misread for a long

sequence of poems, a book
published only after his death—something

to do with the way language breaks
and behaves—a city receding

and growing—something to do
with the way it will not be contained, not even

in chapters. Almost
like poems. It was during the pandemic

that I discovered that the cemetery
I used to cross on my running route

is where an urgent pilgrimage
seemed to take place. Visitors, maybe

students, coming to see—
I wasn't sure

what. I remember thinking—truly, I am not
religious. What was to be found

in this place apart from
stone? Language

was not part of that world, only silence
and a name hovering above the assurance

of numbers—1889-1951—and a few
meters away—the analytic

philosopher and Wittgenstein's translator—
Elizabeth Anscombe—and more

numbers, aiming to shelter from something, perhaps
absence—1919-2001

*

A city cannot stand still or be left
in the darkness. The long spiralling streets

of the night will always be reconstructed
at dawn, the locked field

of a skyline, the rhythm
of loss. *The Vernacular is unstable*

and corruptible—Dante will grant
the most beautiful line of defence

for a word crashing into
another—carrying the wound

of an unsettled thought. A world
that is breaking apart requires

a language—a landscape
for rupture. The small ship

carrying the night before darkness
could not handle the absence of shores. A city

cannot be carried in silence—even
Florence, even a place radiating

with heartbreak, even a street hollowed
by a singular, unbearable

loss. The gift of language
is a beautiful gesture, but only

if practiced—*for nothing is useful*
beyond the amount it is used. Centuries

later, in another attempt against
the structure of chapters, Wittgenstein

will note, *The meaning of a word
is its use in the language.* A prayer

I'll keep carrying with me like a sigh
or an oath. A city cannot be protected

by rumours or letters, it will not be restored
in the realm of a book—even

Florence, even a city haunted
by words. In Dante's

banquet—philosophy is the food
that is served in everyday speech—the bread

that is *made of coarse grain
rather than wheat.*

When I talk about language—Wittgenstein
will note—*I must speak*

*of the language of every day.
So is this language too coarse,*

too material, for what we want to say?
A city will not be erased

by the rupture of language. There is no landscape
ruptured enough to lose hold

of a thought. It was a difficult
autumn—words

disappeared and appeared
like great cities born

out of smoke. That winter, I held onto
Dante—il mio maestro—

held onto
and couldn't let go—

*I, in trying to console myself, found
not only the remedy of my tears but words*

*of authors, fields of knowledge,
and books.*

*

Anger is the most reliable matter—it won't
break—does not need to be looked

after. There's a country—a governing
body—that not only cuts your heart out of your cold, shivering

frame, but does so using your own accent
and language, your own childhood

landscape, your own
tongue. Oh, let me tell you about anger—

...and the despicable, wicked men
of Italy, who debase this precious vernacular.

*

A city will not be protected
by language, but words will keep flooding

the emptied houses, the wide, weeping
landscapes, the nights soaring over the absence

of children running towards a field. Dante
will go back to Florence in 1308—the year

he would learn he'd been banished
for life. *Rejoice, Firenze—*

...for over sea and land and throughout hell
your name outspreads!

Every time I stumble into
this sentence—in the beginning

of *Inferno 26*—something
in me breaks. Anger is the most reliable

matter—and yet, here, it will not stand up
to despair. It was a difficult

autumn. There was something
I learned: it is much easier to traverse

the long hours of night if only one country
pulls your heart out of your body and holds

it like prey, tears its small
membranes apart. Much more difficult

to handle two countries losing
their—I'd like to say *way* or *mind*, but in fact—

heart.
That autumn, people

around me—artists, poets—found joy
in the death of others—those who lived

miles away from the warm-metal hearts
of their screens. It was a difficult

autumn. *Rejoice, Firenze—*
for over sea and land you beat your wings!

*

A city will not be carried in silence. Language
will find its way out of the wreckage

of letters, the absence of courage, the failure
of words to bring

any relief. Time, like theatre, is a matter of distance
turning to action—an unruly prayer

moving, soaring over
the ruins of a field. In Stoppard's *Arcadia*—

the young, fearless heroine
mourns for the loss of knowledge—

All the lost plays of the Athenians… Aristotle's
own library… How can we sleep for grief?

How I wish I had such trust in knowledge
as I have in grief. How I wish

I could sleep. How I wish I could traverse
the cities constructed around the idea of knowledge

without fear. It was a difficult
autumn. The most difficult year. I reached for Dante

because I needed to breathe, needed to be taken
by the dark soaring highway

that links ethics to practice, language
to deeds. All winter

I found myself running in the spiralling evenings
and streets of Florence—a city haunted

by longing, a road leading inwards and outwards,
shaken with grief.

SELF-PORTRAIT AS AUTUMN FIELDS

Any resemblance between the harbour's heightened
theatricality—the riotous turquoise and blue
of the night-falling

snow—and the vast, open highway stretching
under cerulean lightning and cityscape smoke
is accidental, I mean

beautiful—the river turning to frost
was a category error—the water was never
supposed to be held in a palm

like an inanimate object—a tear-shaped
matter, a field in autumn under the aegis of darkness
and snow. I lost the picture

in which I'm running and running
over a bridge made of glass chambers
and smoke. The fire beginning as blue

then light orange, then something I couldn't
explain—not the fire—the fire
was easy—it was what

came after—I wish language was not language—
I remember an airplane—a metallic-heart
engine—a road stretching out

in the autumn-blue smoke—I remember
a river turning multiple rivers, a boat leading
into the heart of an aftermath

snow—I wish language
was easier, much easier to hold
and forget—the word and the matter, the sound

and the picture, the fire and the river—any
resemblance between the wide-open distance
turning sapphire at dusk and the small

paper-lantern held with both palms like a matter
of worth is accidental, I mean difficult, so
difficult to hold.

SNOW LEOPARD AND DARK-IRIS LAKES

Because I'm not sure for how long the main character
is planning to stay—in fact, he's just walked out
to watch the fireworks flowering turquoise and green
as the snow gets heavier and bright—let's just say that for a long-distance
runner and an occasional sprinter, he's one of those erratic treasures
with eyes so intensely cerulean and wild—
one could safely embark on a starship adventure to a far off
planet, knowing those deep, shiny irises will be visible
from space. Two astonishing lakes—
the kind that would turn you into a believer
in distance and play. Soon you will take a crash course
in wild swimming and moon-water
diving, soon you will learn to construct a spaceship
equipped with an advanced telescope lens to help you cope
with the mounting contradiction of velocity and longing
once leaving becomes the inevitable conclusion
of testing out space. You will learn how to bring distant objects
closer—rivers, cities, forests—closer
like the highway spiralling out of a faraway kingdom
you found yourself running around. Back
to our runner—he's based on an ex
of a neighbour who used to be a friend of a colleague
until something (everything) happened—we can study this
forever, but the fireworks are getting louder and the snow
has covered all the lakes, the forests and the villages—
throwing them into a further, harder-to-imagine distance
full of countries wrestling with latitude
and maps. How beautiful
the sky tonight—the way it's shimmering with dark—
and even though the snow is turning into a full-scale
blizzard, you might be able to detect

the woman practicing cartwheel after cartwheel
in the playing field outside. Some describe her
as the girl with the gift for gymnastics and singing
in crowds. Others struggle with her inconvenient tendency
to speak her mind. In any case, you'll recognise
her hard-to-pin-down accent. She's based on three
best friends, two rivers, a long-lost tormented lover, an autumnal
moon poised above a red-oak forest, a skylight
half open to the dark, a snow leopard, a midnight
thunderstorm, an unsent letter, a romantic train guard
holding a rose in a busy train station, a maple leaf on a silver
pavement, a grand piano on the seventh floor, and an entire
country whose borders have been fluctuating
for centuries, and she carries them all
with such burning intensity, there's a very real risk
she'll soon be burning the story she's about to lead, throwing
the ashes into a raging river from some glittering
Eastern European bridge just as the blue autumn
leaves start to blend with the first
signs of snow—a case of a character bigger
than all kinds of storms and sudden weather, stronger
than any towering bridge, wilder than the ever-changing
map of Eastern Europe before, between and after
the war/s, and while I know
you'd rather head back to those delicious
blue lakes—and I'm totally with you on that—I must
introduce you to another character, the one who's rarely
running late. You might want to reach
for a few bracing cocktails before we kick off. Are you ready
to defy distance, matter, logics, the spectacular
fields of applied mathematics and theoretical physics
and watch how a brief course of events
turn into a chaos indefensibly long? In short,
please welcome our comrade—a devoted, fervent

socialist. I suspect he'd appreciate it if you stood up
when he enters the room. What a way to land back
in the wonder that is—say—England in the years leading
to 2019. Where shall we begin? Outside, a lightning storm
is spiralling the streets into a sequence of luminous
and pitch-dark scenes. As for our comrade, right—
another drink? Yes, he's a narcissist—you've
got it—yes, he's a little bit of a misogynist. Sure,
he's upper-middle class—but only
in this story, which is surreal *and* fictional—Everybody
Calm Down—he's based on five high-school friends, several
pious atheists, I mean—saints, twenty-six
hangovers, seven didactic lectures, the longest
summer heatwave recorded to date, the magnetic theatricality
of protest politics, a Sunday in Trafalgar Square, a promising
vegan deli, two pleasant pubs somewhere faraway
in the English countryside, a rose
as a symbol of—wait for it—dissent, a significant
proportion of the UK poetry scene, and a few
of my worst nightmares during those years, in which
for the first time, for some reason, I found myself running
in the streets of 1930s Krakow as if there was something or someone
I had to see. The massive distraction that is politics
has led us astray, yet again, from those deep beautiful
lakes, although I'm not sure the distraction is politics, it is
something else—not history, not ideology, not even
the fast luminous horses of populism soaring above
every river and bridge, nor the cries of sainthood
in the age of victimhood—no, it is something
else, darker than these. Although in this version,
the comrade will turn into a painter—an artist who believes
in Art for its own sake. We'll come back to this
later. For now, the mountains are covered with snow, the rivers
are flowing with shimmering frost. Listen, you are on a mission

to embark on a starship towards the deepest blue
lakes. You're focused and impatient—fasten
your seatbelt and don't be distracted—only a few more
characters to go: meet Dora, an uptight cello player with a tendency
to declare open season on cats. There's Val—a young
professional with a considerable past, Remi—French, Laura,
an Italian living in exile (her words), and finally—
a messenger. Yep, a real one. I'm still looking into
the practicalities of a downright divine
intervention, but in the meantime—I'd be up for testing
the ground. Is anyone pregnant? Is anyone up for
rolling in a field naked? Until we sort out
these questions, let me take you on a winter break
far away in Zakopane—a resort town in southern
Poland—somewhere
between 1922 and 1927. Let me know if you can see
the girl playing in the snow—she's strong
and muscular—there—you can tell it's her
by her wide, palest-green eyes, there's something
rebellious in the way she lets go
of her mother's hand, lifting her younger
brother up in the air, chasing
her cousins like a furious leopard. I had no idea
she could cartwheel like this. I'm not sure I recognise
her confidence, her uncontrolled laughter, her incredible
smile. She's stronger than anyone
around her—yes, I recognise that. I don't think she notices
me, and if she does, she could never imagine
being a grandmother one day. It would make her cartwheel
out of this fragile picture, catch the first train
and throw up. I want to tell her don't let go
of your mother's hand. I want to tell her you don't understand
what's about to happen—you're not stronger
or bigger than this place and sudden weather, the country

you will run away from is so much larger
than you—it won't even notice
when you're gone, neither
will it care, it won't bother to write down
your parents' and grandparents' names, the entirety
of your cousins and friends, there will be no
hand left to hold onto, no addresses, it will be up to you
to memorise these traces of places and names, and yes—
good luck with that. I want to tell her, listen—don't take it the wrong
way, but could you please go? I'm trying
to write a story with actual fireworks—I have a brilliant
set of characters, it was supposed to be
funny. Have you heard the one
about the zealous socialist believing in Art for its own sake? Me
neither! I'm in the process of devising a divine
intervention—a Socialist, a Saint and a Populist walk into
a Stoppard play—something along these lines or
temperament, there's supposed to be a full-blown tension
between Dora and Remi—the latter arrived two hours
ago, and already attracts a hell of a lot of attention,
there's a strong possibility that someone becomes miraculously
pregnant, even though I haven't worked out
why Laura is in exile, why Val is rereading the same
letter while chain-smoking all night, there are some unresolved
issues with flying cello strings and a few alarmed
cats, but instead of sorting them out I'm pushing
the door open and walking outside, raising the night
like a glass—holding this fear like a country
changing its mind or its borders, a snowstorm erasing
all traces and maps. I want to tell her, look—
there are two delicious cerulean lakes my readers
would really appreciate if I could finally
lead them to. It was a promise I made—not only to them
but to myself—that I shall not be distracted—

and I've just completed the most elegant starship
fitted with telescopes, cameras, long-distance
fire and snow, you see—there's this blue-eyed absolute
treasure—he was supposed to symbolise the aesthetically-pleasing
tension between a growing, unbearable distance
and the shattering impracticality of creative
attention—he's based on an ex of a neighbour who
used to be, well—the short story
is—would you mind taking back your, our
history and placing it on some random steep mountain or a faraway
bridge, maybe drop it into a raging Eastern European river by mistake,
would you stop repeating all those cousins' and friends' and
parents' names, I'm building a starship, I'm taking us
back to where it feels safest, I'm taking us back
to the lakes.

THE PAIN OR THE PIANO-TUNING

After Wittgenstein, *Philosophical Investigations*,
§666 and §678

I

Someone is playing in the next room. In the distance, a road
leading towards a lake under a high-wire

moon: a perilous sky—a form of knowledge—to run
along the river and break into tears—yes, I can carry

a word like a small creature of night, I can measure out
speed against gestures of sound, train memory

into a stop-motion device, build a room
as a flight-capable machine—

the air new and attentive to light, the sky made of irresolute
stars holding onto the moon-soaring

fields. A form of knowledge—a new blue
emerging intact—wide-open, empirical and dark. Yes, in fact—

*Imagine that you were in pain and were simultaneously
hearing a piano being tuned in the next room.*

II

Someone is playing in the next room. A new sky
emerging intact—an exterior with streetlight and high-wire

night—a form of knowledge—a sketch of two chambers
in the upper-blue dark: two moving

images, two mountains breaking apart, two sunsets
testing out rivers flowing towards the impulse of light. Imagine

that you were in pain and simultaneously—two cities
emerge out of the water, ready for flight. Yes,

I can carry a word like a small creature of sound, train memory
into a lightproof device, draw landscapes out of water, more

water and high-ceilinged clouds—a wave of knowledge
or a wave of sorrow—a form of holding

onto the dark—a point of leaving—*or a way of shutting one's eyes*
which might be called 'looking into oneself'.

A wave of sorrow. A word for studying, soaring into
the dark—a new moon emerging in flight—a light-storing

machine. To run along the river—yes, I can hold onto
a tear like a small creature of glass—I have done this

all year. There are always two chambers in the upper-blue
dark, two pianos, two opposite rivers, two moons battling

night—a force of knowledge, or a form of holding
onto a sound—someone is playing in the next room, an exterior

with thunder and high-ceilinged dark. A form of looking
into oneself which might be called leaving or being

attentive to the small ripples of night. *What does this meaning (the pain,
or the piano-tuning) consist in?* What does a sigh flowing

towards a sound? A wave of sorrow or a word for longing—
a field of attention drawing in light. Something like light.

UN AMOUR DÉSESPÉRÉ

ALL HAULERS

Conversation with Rimbaud, *Le Bateau ivre*

Comme je descendais des Fleuves impassibles,
Je ne me sentis plus guidé par les haleurs:
Des Peaux-Rouges criards les avaient pris pour cibles
Les ayant cloués nus aux poteaux de couleurs.

> It is always the water. The rain sets the evening in motion—
> the streetlamps throw light like metallic blue knives. All haulers
> are couriers of motion. If I'm guided by water
> let it be a river as furious as this.

J'étais insoucieux de tous les équipages,
Porteur de blés flamands ou de cotons anglais.
Quand avec mes haleurs ont fini ces tapages,
Les Fleuves m'ont laissé descendre où je voulais.

> Indifference: to be free. The eye is a chamber, a field
> of blue lightnings. The harbour, an uproar of darkening
> stars. All haulers are couriers of water, all rivers
> are careless and flowing, forming new maps.

Dans les clapotements furieux des marées,
Moi, l'autre hiver, plus sourd que les cerveaux d'enfants,
Je courus! Et les Péninsules démarrées
N'ont pas subi tohu-bohus plus triomphants.

> Genesis 1. Some translations read *Tohu va-Vohu* as *without
> form*. Others as *void*. Others as both. Beginnings are messy. Choice
> is exhausting like the naming of water, each river
> and source. *And darkness was upon the face of the deep.*

La tempête a béni mes éveils maritimes.
Plus léger qu'un bouchon j'ai dansé sur les flots
Qu'on appelle rouleurs éternels de victimes,
Dix nuits, sans regretter l'œil niais des falots!

Night vigils. There's a phone ringing in a far-off flat
like a neon-blue flame, some music mixing nightfall with fireworks
and light-sapphire rain. Somewhere a police car
with a spiralling eye circles a lake.

Plus douce qu'aux enfants la chair des pommes sûres,
L'eau verte pénétra ma coque de sapin
Et des taches de vins bleus et des vomissures
Me lava, dispersant gouvernail et grappin.

Apples and childhood—it always works. The promise
of knowledge, of urgent beginnings. Today I'm thinking
of a sky raining blue wine as an exercise
in hope. If you introduce an apple in the first act...

Et dès lors, je me suis baigné dans le Poème
De la Mer, infusé d'astres, et lactescent,
Dévorant les azurs verts; où, flottaison blême
Et ravie, un noyé pensif parfois descend;

To throw a stone like an incomplete thought
into the darkening mirror of volatile stars. To dive
and bring it back—I'm not sure how that works—water
and depth, water and water—

Où, teignant tout à coup les bleuités, délires
Et rhythmes lents sous les rutilements du jour,
Plus fortes que l'alcool, plus vastes que nos lyres,
Fermentent les rousseurs amères de l'amour!

Stronger than alcohol, louder than a night turning soundwaves
and fire. All haulers are couriers of errors. Don't mistake
water for depth. So much better to mistake it for love—
a delirious flow under the bitter blossoming dark.

Je sais les cieux crevant en éclairs, et les trombes
Et les ressacs et les courants: je sais le soir,
L'Aube exaltée ainsi qu'un peuple de colombes,
Et j'ai vu quelquefois ce que l'homme a cru voir!

I know winters: dawns exhausted by the promise
of fire and snow. I know the city heavy with silver-pink
fog, the lakes overfilling with ice and blue glass, the rain
cutting through smoke. And I know the sunrise burning with dark.

J'ai vu le soleil bas, taché d'horreurs mystiques,
Illuminant de longs figements violets,
Pareils à des acteurs de drames très-antiques
Les flots roulant au loin leurs frissons de volets!

From the ceiling, a yellow circle dips and settles, almost
touching the ground. There's a lake made of metal-blue feathers,
and a small paper boat in the ultra-violet light. In a film,
a child draws and redraws the heart as a four-chambered map.

J'ai rêvé la nuit verte aux neiges éblouies,
Baiser montant aux yeux des mers avec lenteurs,
La circulation des sèves inouïes,
Et l'éveil jaune et bleu des phosphores chanteurs!

On the stage, a model of a heart made of blue copper
and brass. The chambers are lanterns pulsing warm yellow
lights. It is snowing. The lake has vanished, the paper boat turned into
a map. A storm is approaching. All dreamers are carriers of night.

J'ai suivi, des mois pleins, pareille aux vacheries
Hystériques, la houle à l'assaut des récifs,
Sans songer que les pieds lumineux des Maries
Pussent forcer le mufle aux Océans poussifs!

Hysterical: for an entire blooming month. Coughing blue algae
and salt. The new-towering mountain was only a castle
made of whirlpool and coral-reef maps. Theatrical: for an entire
night. I'm drinking the full moon as a warm volatile heart.

J'ai heurté, savez-vous, d'incroyables Florides
Mêlant aux fleurs des yeux de panthères à peaux
D'hommes! Des arcs-en-ciel tendus comme des brides
Sous l'horizon des mers, à de glauques troupeaux!

Flowers are distractions. Rainbows and panthers
are full-on distractions. Dreams, yes—interruptions. Gardens
and apples—how shall I put it? Everything
is a distraction. Childhood, childhood—

J'ai vu fermenter les marais énormes, nasses
Où pourrit dans les joncs tout un Léviathan!
Des écroulements d'eaux au milieu des bonaces
Et les lointains vers les gouffres cataractant!

In the beginning there was childhood. Chaos
was mistaken for choice. There was distance and more distance
but no doors. A river was turning into a map, a city
into a memory, a sea monster circling the ruins of a boat.

Glaciers, soleils d'argent, flots nacreux, cieux de braises!
Échouages hideux au fond des golfes bruns
Où les serpents géants dévorés des punaises
Choient, des arbres tordus, avec de noirs parfums!

On the stage, the boat is a metallic-blue spine, the lake is a relic—
the trace of a glacier. Take a picture of the silver suns, the ceiling
burning into orange embers. The dream devours
the seafloor, the garden, the serpent.

J'aurais voulu montrer aux enfants ces dorades
Du flot bleu, ces poissons d'or, ces poissons chantants.
—Des écumes de fleurs ont bercé mes dérades
Et d'ineffables vents m'ont ailé par instants.

Children, when they said the aquarium is open to the public
they meant closed. The beautiful blue is locked inside metal
and glass. The seahorse and sunfish are under construction. Let me
show you how to carry a storm in a box.

Parfois, martyr lassé des pôles et des zones,
La mer dont le sanglot faisait mon roulis doux
Montait vers moi ses fleurs d'ombre aux ventouses jaunes
Et je restais, ainsi qu'une femme à genoux...

—Almost there, part ocean part land: I'm an Other—a floating
chamber, the woman on her knees holding onto the tenacity
of shadow flowers, the vanity of water testing gravity and flight. All
haulers are couriers of shadows. All chambers, carriers of sound—

Presque île, ballottant sur mes bords les querelles
Et les fientes d'oiseaux clabaudeurs aux yeux blonds.
Et je voguais, lorsqu'à travers mes liens frêles
Des noyés descendaient dormir, à reculons!

Those dark birds with yellow eyes—I have sent them away
and named them *memories*. When they come back, they fly
backwards to sleep—turning nights into castles of fire, chambers
of blue-lightning fields, turning distance to maps.

Or moi, bateau perdu sous les cheveux des anses,
Jeté par l'ouragan dans l'éther sans oiseau,
Moi dont les Monitors et les voiliers des Hanses
N'auraient pas repêché la carcasse ivre d'eau;

You are only sixteen and already you write: *I, a boat lost.*
At sixteen I followed the boy carrying a canoe
on his shoulders as if it were a light choice. The air
was volatile and thickening with salt.

Libre, fumant, monté de brumes violettes,
Moi qui trouais le ciel rougeoyant comme un mur
Qui porte, confiture exquise aux bons poètes,
Des lichens de soleil et des morves d'azur,

—I'd vote for the smoke, the violet fog, the sky turning sand
and red stone. All haulers are couriers of motion and I'm trying,
I'm trying to hold onto the water, the river, the silver
suns burning with snow—

Qui courais, taché de lunules électriques,
Planche folle, escorté des hippocampes noirs,
Quand les juillets faisaient crouler à coups de triques
Les cieux ultramarins aux ardents entonnoirs;

The stage is lit with electric-blue moons. Finally,
the city. Finally, electricity. The sea is theatrical, the stars
made of tempered-red glass. Summer is always too much. The sky
bruised with ultramarine, the lakes heavy with light.

Moi qui tremblais, sentant geindre à cinquante lieues
Le rut des Béhémots et les Maelstroms épais,
Fileur éternel des immobilités bleues,
Je regrette l'Europe aux anciens parapets!

In another country, the phone is still ringing, a car
is still circling a lake like an unbroken thought, a dream feeding
the night with a moon warm and burning, an island
constructed out of more islands, more sunsets, more storms—

J'ai vu des archipels sidéraux! et des îles
Dont les cieux délirants sont ouverts au vogueur:
—Est-ce en ces nuits sans fonds que tu dors et t'exiles,
Million d'oiseaux d'or, ô future Vigueur?

A constellation of archipelagos: phone calls, new cities, some
letters, addresses, lost notes. Perhaps you wanted the water
to carve out its own direction, offer new forms. All haulers
are sea-wanderers, I get that, carriers of home.

Mais, vrai, j'ai trop pleuré! Les Aubes sont navrantes.
Toute lune est atroce et tout soleil amer:
L'âcre amour m'a gonflé de torpeurs enivrantes.
Ô que ma quille éclate! Ô que j'aille à la mer!

Moons are atrocious. I couldn't agree more. Suns
are bitter, dark silver and cold. Love is acrid and swollen, light
is intoxicating, apples are misleading, cities are made of warm
misunderstandings, sunsets are false. Dawns are heartbreaking.

Si je désire une eau d'Europe, c'est la flache
Noire et froide où vers le crépuscule embaumé
Un enfant accroupi plein de tristesse, lâche
Un bateau frêle comme un papillon de mai.

In the penultimate scene, a child sends a paper boat
into the lake. Remember the apple? The moon was a distraction,
the storm was a toss-up between memory and function, the garden
was made of overrated sanctions—beautiful and cold.

Je ne puis plus, baigné de vos langueurs, ô lames,
Enlever leur sillage aux porteurs de cotons,
Ni traverser l'orgueil des drapeaux et des flammes,
Ni nager sous les yeux horribles des pontons.

I'll go for the city's theatrical hybris, the traffic at night. All cities
are couriers of motion. All lanterns, carriers of dusk. You will go on
to write *Metropolitan,* trading rivers for new rivers and streets. All
haulers are carriers of wonder. If I'm guided by water let it be this.

UN AMOUR DÉSESPÉRÉ

An evening like this, to carry Rimbaud's *Ville*
in my palms—my dear, unreliable, beating city
and sky, my emblem of night. *La morale et la langue*
sont réduites à leur plus simple expression, enfin!

Great waves will be crashing on the dark-sapphire shore
of this city at night. New furies will blossom and open
like blue wounds in the coal-fractured shadow of stars—
notre ombre des bois, notre nuit d'été! A revelation—

that it was possible—to love like this, even here, even
in this nightfall traversed by strangers—*ces millions de gens*
qui n'ont pas besoin de se connaître—to love like this—

to be so desperate—to watch the spectres breathing smoke
into the streets preoccupied with crime and death—*et tout mon cœur*—
and care so much, care so desperately for this place.

UNE GAÎTÉ DIVINE

To be devoted like this: put up a theatre stage. *Exilé ici,*
j'ai eu une scène où jouer... To play under the new turmoil
of sky turning rain. *Je suis un inventeur*—you write in *Vies*
before declaring yourself *un musicien même,* the one

who holds *la clef de l'amour*—yes. To invent the moon
as a bright invocation. Sure. To hold onto time—*J'essaye*
de m'émouvoir au souvenir de l'enfance mendiante. I'd love
to learn this: how to fall into the polemic of dream

landscape, a river of sleep. There was always something
you couldn't escape. The city. Childhood. Divine happiness
was not one of those things. *Je ne regrette pas ma vieille part*

de gaîté divine. Joy? Really? But your poem's already taken
me towards an attic, a nocturnal feast, *un vieux passage à Paris*
where you carry the night like a field of science. To study like this.

LE MALHEUR A ÉTÉ MON DIEU

Conversation with Rimbaud, *Une saison en enfer*,
opening section

«Jadis, si je me souviens bien, ma vie était un festin
où s'ouvraient tous les cœurs, où tous les vins coulaient.

If I remember well, memory, back then
was all water. The hearts were open

like the floating chambers of a city deserted—
broken and open and howling with storms.

Un soir, j'ai assis la Beauté sur mes genoux.
—Et je l'ai trouvée amère.—Et je l'ai injuriée.

Beauty, if I remember correctly, was supposed
to protect me—to hold me close. I think

I get it: I was always the one meant to be injured
but unbroken, beautiful but not to the point

it risked uninvited attention, the conquering of fire
towards a wild direction, the false promise of dawn.

Je me suis armé contre la justice.
Je me suis enfui. Ô sorcières, ô misère, ô haine,
c'est à vous que mon trésor a été confié!

At the gate of the city, the country, the court
I defended Beauty as if it was a real, unchanging

matter. Armed with memory, I recited the trial
of night out of dust and dusk paper, if

I remember correctly, singing was very
much a way to remember—remember

better, remember fully. O beauty, O poverty, O
shivering pain, O dust-treasure of memory.

Je parvins à faire s'évanouir dans mon esprit
toute l'espérance humaine. Sur toute joie pour l'étrangler
j'ai fait le bond sourd de la bête féroce.

If I remember correctly, at some point, memory
turned into a film—a wild beast forming

out of the fracture of night, the full force
of longing. There was no beauty, no country, only

a past. All human hope, all potentiality—
I wanted to find it and hold it close—all

suffering, all shattered dawns—I wanted
it all and to have nothing to do with it.

J'ai appelé les bourreaux pour, en périssant, mordre la crosse
de leurs fusils. J'ai appelé les fléaux, pour m'étouffer
avec le sable, le sang. Le malheur a été mon dieu.

Sorrow was my true source—my new brilliant
God—sure, but also: theatre, also

joy. At the town square—like the greatest
of amateurs—I summoned

the executioners to the stage—yes—
the grand provocateurs

of youth. But if I remember correctly, Beauty
was already dead. The silence

of blood as it ran through the sand—I remember
it all—the flutter of cry as it broke into air—

*Je me suis allongé dans la boue. Je me suis séché
à l'air du crime. Et j'ai joué de bons tours à la folie.*

This is what I know: how water
has to recede in order for anything else

to survive—words on paper, pictures, letters,
but not memories. Memories can swim

even when broken. Memories can play crazy
tricks on this dark season of water—

Et le printemps m'a apporté l'affreux rire de l'idiot.

Yes. There were always those
who blossomed in spring.

*Or, tout dernièrement m'étant trouvé sur le point
de faire le dernier couac! j'ai songé à rechercher la clef
du festin ancien, où je reprendrais peut-être appétit.*

The code to the ancient banquet—if
I remember correctly—I seized it

from the still-beating engine
of a ship drowning faster in night turning

flight—a deep-dreaming hunter. I held it
like a weapon, an emblem

of lust—a last cry with no private meaning
but fear. A season in hell, i.e., hunger.

La charité est cette clef.—Cette inspiration
prouve que j'ai rêvé!

That spring, I was always
dreaming. There was something about not wanting

to wake up, not wanting to leave
what's not finished.

«Tu resteras hyène, etc...,» se récrie le démon
qui me couronna de si aimables pavots. «Gagne la mort
avec tous tes appétits, et ton égoïsme et tous les péchés capitaux.»

I was always the one meant to be injured
but unbroken—a creature not taken with beauty

but the wandering, strange structure
of motion. The false crown of poppies

flew from my head like sudden blue
feathers. The demon of youth held me close

with no promise—all selfishness, all
sin, all wasting of dawns and dark

tenderness—I wanted it all and to have
nothing to do with it—an impulse of sleep.

Ah! j'en ai trop pris: —Mais, cher Satan, je vous en conjure,
une prunelle moins irritée!

Dear Satan, don't look away, I am standing
right here. Dear amateur, dear skilful

provocateur—dear night turning dust and fast
theatre, dear sorrow—my dear brilliant

divinity and sin—by now you must know how to capture
the waves and dark waste of my memory—

et en attendant les quelques petites lâchetés en retard,

—sorry, but if I remember
correctly—there was no waiting

room large enough for all the cowards
to fit in—

vous qui aimez dans l'écrivain l'absence des facultés
descriptives ou instructives,

Look, I have taken my memory—my incomplete
film—and torn each river, each hideous ribbon

of spring, each public and private exhibition
of my heart—each theatre

stage and improvised scene, each declaration
of night turning infinite field—each fear—

*je vous détache ces quelques hideux feuillets
de mon carnet de damné.*

If I remember well, memory, back then,
was all water—my hearts were open, open

and locked like the flooded chambers of a city
taken, shaken by thoughts. Dear reader, dear accidental

carrier of words, dear holder of hearts
shattered and closed—please handle with care

when you tear up the sheets—the vast, changing
fields and great shields—of these notes.

FILM

Brilliant. Now do sorrow.
—Tom Stoppard, *The Hard Problem*

The film begins with a metal-blue moon suspended
over a stage. There's an airplane taking off and a teenager
smoking next to a magazine stand—somewhere

on a green island a tree battling wind, a ship testing
the moon in the map of a lake, a girl breaking a lock
with the strike of a high heel, the film begins

with a woman calling a taxi, holding onto her fifth
cup of espresso that turns into the seventh—the ninth
in the following scene. Somewhere, September, a girl throws

a book into a red messenger-bag. She carries the moon
in the store of her phone, running to catch the final night
train—the phone like a sword or a night-burning

match. Maybe she's wearing a red dress, maybe
an off trend, oversized trench. The film begins
with a bridge turning into a river, a rainstorm, a flock

of dark geese. Somewhere, it's summer, a boy catches
a fish from a fresh-water stream, a girl measures a heart
with the flick of two fists, a ring floats on the warmth

of a late-August lake, a taxi breaks out of the highway
before it arrives at the wrong address. The film begins
with a plane taking off in the lightest of rain. In a different

country—midsummer party—a waiter is serving blue fire
on porcelain plates. Somewhere, December, the final
ten seconds—the sky turning soundscapes and arrows

of coral-reef stars. There's a story I once disappeared
into: a child chasing a storm, a ring floats on a lake—
I remember reading and swimming and not wanting

to come back. The film begins with an orchestra
and a forest and a wide sapphire field. On a train,
a girl studies a play on moral philosophy, the problem

of consciousness, the circle of grief. How to do
sorrow. Her red-messenger bag is thrown on the floor
like a sliced-open heart. Somewhere, November, a driver

is lost in a foreign-land snow, a woman studies
her phone's broken signal, the pulse in her wrist, the word
in her throat. I remember running and running

and not caring to look back. The film begins
with a disco party on the midsummer shore. Maybe
God. Surely physics or something to do with what

we don't know, I mean God. Somewhere, 30,000 feet
above sea level—a recorded message reminds
the passengers that smoking is a concept worth

dreaming about mid-air. I forgot to mention—
there's always a split screen—a wave following
a wave. On one side—childhood. On the other, everything

else. One screen features blue fire. The other, a waiter
serving the fire to the ravenous guests. One screen
features a kingfisher, the other—an airplane circling

the map of a foreign-land word. The film begins
with a woman having to make a choice. The book
or the nightfall, the sword or the torch, the flight

or the highway, the script or the snow. I have learnt
that a woman must always begin, must always
hold onto a choice—the word or the picture, the real

or the heightened, the myth or the promise. One screen
features a child, the other—a ring flying into
the smoke. One screen features a pram, the other—

another. The stage or the sentence, the door or the lock,
the cry or the contract, the word or the court. The film
begins with the only possible way to begin—

each movement, each sorrow, each word—in the beginning
there was a woman put into action. In the beginning
there was a woman having to make a choice.

AFFOGATO

For God's sake, Bernard, you haven't established
Byron was even here!
—Tom Stoppard, *Arcadia*

December, and the stars are glasses of dark
ice, like burning blue coal—like a city reeling
from a snow-flowering night. In the morning

I go for a run. Later I'm back in the play
that turns space into multiple times—the strange
world of chaos theory, the inevitability of sex

scandals, the poet as an interloper, trading darkness
for fire but never on stage—like a burning possibility
eager to challenge the beauty or fury

of taking shape. Proof, like a nightfall fractured
with stars. Proof, like a volatile city. I'm thinking
of a floating opera—somewhere in the map

of the mind—the poet as conceptual art, ruling
the waves of a wild speculation. December, the streets
are turning, moving apart. Somewhere, snow burns

on a volcanic landscape, forests consumed by the heartbeats
of fire. In the morning, I go for a run. Later—
I have to go back to eight years ago

in the Financial Times: *It's fighting against*
the second principle of thermodynamics. It's a desperate
tentative attempt to stop time. This was the answer

the physicist gave to the question: *What
is your favourite dessert?* I like desperate tentative
attempts. I like trying and failing

to stop time. December, the moon almost touches
the water like a light provocation or low hanging
prey. I like Affogatos. I like running, running

between newspapers and plays. Somewhere, a ship
navigates the vanishing landscape, a poet walks out
of a fictional scene as if leaving a sigh

in an incomplete sentence. Proof, a kinetic fixed
agent. On the stage—two couples are moving in circles
in opposite directions, a play taking form

like a structural question, a play *suffused with the dark
implications, the irreversible enervations of the second
law of thermodynamics.* Proof, a night reeling

from an approximation of snow opposite fire. A poet
crossing the night as if drawing a landscape—a city
consumed by the fuel and the flutter of darkening stars.

LOVE, AN ACCIDENT IN A SUBSTANCE

For C: After Dante, *Vita Nuova*

I

Tonight the moon is excessive, a flareup
of hovering light. The fields radiate darkness—

blue and silver-blue fragments of tarmac
and clouds. Maybe this is what it means, driving

the roads of this country without knowing
where to arrive. In the *Vita Nuova*, each room

turns into a wide-opening scene—the sky
falling and falling and never stopping—

never reaching the ground. *It's as if in that world—*
the preface tells me—*every experience*

deserves to be told twice—first
in prose, then poetry. Love as a heat centre

in which every incident starts
with a vision, a dream—a hell

of hallucination—a city where every street
leads into the vast field of a grief

landscape. *What love was doing to me*—this—
this should have been the title

of this epic short heartache of poetry
and prose—*Quale Amor mi facea*—

had I been the editor of this nothing
but shivering and grief-stricken

storm. Instead, it's a line that appears only
later—in chapter 16—almost

as an afterthought—*What love was doing
to me*—a question of tension, a gesture

to which the reader, at this point
can only respond—yes—

I, too, have walked in the rain for an entire
year like a complete idiot, I, too, cried

in public places with no shame or self-worth—
I, too, *was struck with a desire*

to write a poem. Outside, the city
keeps happening as if in a film—morning

and then evening, the inescapable
storm—first prose, then poetry—

maybe this is what it means, driving all night
without reaching home. I, too, needed an entire city

to be grieving with me—each streetlight
and building, each broken rooftop and half-open

evening, each person running to catch
the last bus in the snow, each visitor caught

in the wrong train station, the wrong
conversation, each

commuter clutching onto the light
of their phones. *I would surely make them weep*

before they left the city—this—this
should have been the title of this epic epicentre

of passion and loss—a title that would firmly
place the writer at the city gates—

an entity in charge of traffic and emotion—
I would surely make them weep

before they left the city. A statement full
of confidence and heartache—a writer

struggling to breathe between each
note. Tonight the moon is unacceptable—

a ring of blue and purple—there's too much
beauty for these breathing fields of darkness

to take in—too much of this nightfall
turning speed. Maybe this is what it means, driving

the roads of this landscape and not knowing
where to begin. First, love. Then,

grief. It is always this way—always in this
direction. I would surely make them weep

before they left the city—*Io li pur farei piangere*
anzi ch'elli uscissero di questa cittade.

II

Everything is happening at once—the moon
is floating, throbbing in the water

like a shattered, magnifying
glass. The river takes off from the unsteady

ground like a torn ribbon of light, and each
road leading inwards and outwards—

towards the vacant, broken centre
of the heart. Maybe this is what it means—

driving the fields of this country
and not reaching the vast, open station

of night. Everything
is happening and happening

fast—love and the moving entity
of lust—*I wrote down*

what I had seen in my sleep. This, this
could be the title. A vision of a heart

taken out, being fed as a movement
of hunger—love and the want

of respite. It's as if, in this place—
each incident deserves to be dreamt

twice. The heart and the craving
of heart. The dream and the aching of dream

carried into the light. *I wrote down*
what I had seen in my sleep—

Scrissi a loro ciò ch'io avea nel mio sonno
veduto. It is always like this, always

in this direction. First, love. Then—
walking and walking

this wide landscape—the floating geography
of sleep—a matter of falling, the ground

turning into a flight—
maybe this is what it means, driving

the roads of this landscape and not even trying
to wake up.

III

It's as if, in this place, every picture
demands to be drawn twice. First the dream, then

the account. And each line, each question, opens and flows
in the same direction. *My only reply*

would have been: "Love." Where have you been?
Beatrice. Is it still snowing? Beatrice. Why are you running

outside in this weather? Beatrice. Have you forgotten
something? Beatrice. Are you actually out

of your mind? *La mia risponsione sarebbe stata solamente:*
"Amore." Could you trace the locked, changing colour

of night? Beatrice. Have you noticed how ice
turns to fire in the dark? Beatrice. If a city is wanting

of one person, will snow start falling and falling
because it is missing the ground? Beatrice. Beatrice. Beatrice—

IV

Tonight the city is floating against
the darkening landscape, the sky carrying a chamber

of high thunder and lights. The moon
is outrageous: a shivering

blue turning ice. There are so many ways
to be desperate. *I am seized with such*

a powerful desire to see her
that it kills and destroys

whatever might rise up against it
in my memory. The memory of rain

like a private soundtrack. The memory
of light like an open-air

film. Maybe this is what it means, driving
the night of this landscape

and not managing to sleep. The sky
turning fire and snow

as if careless.
Desire that Kills and Destroys—this

should be the title—written in neon purple
on a highway billboard overlooking

the full structure of traffic at dawn, the air
testing smoke in the rivers of light—

Un Disiderio che Uccide e Distrugge—
yes—the city as memory film

where each building—each incident—
is slowly then quickly devastated—first

in prose, then poetry—then in a harbour action
scene—it is always this way, always

in this direction. *Love as potentiality*
transformed into actuality—yes—

I need to go back to this section
in chapter 20, where each possibility

opens and grows into a field of live
action—even when words

are still being tested—the memory
of sky like a free falling

curtain. The memory of rivers
like an unsettled screen. First the dream, then

the misapprehension: everything
is happening and happening

twice. Everything, sure, except
life. Maybe this is what it means, driving

the roads of this landscape and not knowing
how to remember, how to remember enough.

V

Tonight I'm driving the fields of the city
as each street turns into a river

of sound. There is something about snow—
I'm never quite sure

how it begins—never know how
to react—a matter of holding it in against

darkness. A matter of floating— not
falling—apart. What love is doing to me.

VI

Tonight the city is absent. The river
is stretching against the locked exhibition

of sky. The moon is distasteful—a fissure
of light against orange-blue

fire. Maybe this is what it means, driving
and driving and not wanting

to slow down. The sun has grown
dark, the colours of stars *made me think*

that they were weeping—
a vision of death before the carrying

of night—a rehearsal
in mourning—the stage-directions of rain

turning into the ruptured geography
of sound. It's as if in this place, each chamber

carries its own unreliable
heart. It is always this way, always in this

direction. First the dream, then the misleading
relief of a day breaking out—

and a few chapters later—as if light
always cut into the disquieting glass

of another dream soundscape—
The usual tremor of the heart. Yes—

this should be the title—*Lo tremore usato
nel cuore*—a title that would point the writer

back towards the city gates—the crowds
of pilgrims flow like broken, breathing

waves, the sky initiates the theatre
of sleep—maybe this is what it means,

driving the ruins of this landscape
and not managing to grieve.

Tonight the moon is volatile blue in the absence
of snow. *For love is not in itself a substance,*

but rather an accident in a substance.
There are so many ways to get lost

in this sentence—walk in the darkening streets
of a city astounded with light taken

by rain. The vast growing fields of the night
lay under invisible stars like new water—

Ché Amore non è per sé sí come sustanzia,
ma è uno accidente in sustanzia—

it will take me years, years, to walk back
to this sentence and break it apart—a field

of locked water under disquieting sky, but now
I'm thinking—whatever it means—yes—

it's as if in this place, each accident
demands to be tried twice. Each possibility

turned actuality. Each introspection
forming into a theatrical night. Years

later—on mount Purgatorio—the storm
carrying fog on the Terrace of Wrath—love—

the reader will be told—is in fact
of two separate kinds. The mind moves

like fire—*the mind, which is created
quick to love*—the mind travels in two

directions— *L'animo, ch'è creato
ad amar presto*—it will take me years

to climb down from this difficult mountain
back to the city of loss

and grief landscape. Love, an accident
in a substance, where each physical matter

turns into the fraction and fast movement
of words. Maybe this is what it means, driving

away from this city, driving and crying
and not managing to hold.

VIII

Tonight the city is wanting. The moon
is exceptional—an absence

of light in the incoming storm. It is always
this way. First, the city locked

and deserted—then the writer
stepping into the vacant town

centre, carrying each ruin
like a new-forming thought. Love

as a matter of language, of what's left
to hold close. Wow—Dante—

it is chapter 25 that keeps calling
me back as if there was something I need

to look after, a word
I forgot. The poets arrive at this city

of wreckage, addressing *inanimate objects*
as if they had sense and reason, making them

speak to each other… not only real things
but unreal things… It's as if in this place, each

fragment deserves to be breathed
into life. Each broken centre

of the heart, each moon trying out beauty
as a way of survival—a matter

of a fight. There's a story to be told—
in which I would speak weepingly

of her for whom great grief destroyed
my soul. Everything

is happening at once—the lamentation
and evocation, the dark apprehension and tension

of love. First in prose, then poetry, then—
life. Life—really, should have happened

twice. Even when shattered. Especially
when shattered. First in the original

tongue—*per cui tanto dolore*
era fatto distruggitore dell'anima mia—

then in translation, the way each moon
looks after light—*for whom great grief*

destroyed my soul. Then, the inevitable
interpretation: grief—a destroyer

of the heart. Grief, the vast breathing
movement of words—

I would surely make them weep
before they left the city—

maybe this is what it means, driving and
driving away from the ruins and new moons—new

life reigning over this shivering-sky scenery—
and not managing to leave.

PLAYING FIELDS

I

Call it geography: how to hold and draw
directions, cut a map into water

and land, measure time in units of running
or flying divided by irregular speed

or sharp palpitations, hold onto
the cold purpose of rivers, the strange presence

of stars—I'd like to think
this is how memory works—a blue slate

on a silver pavement, a bell ringing and ringing
from the ruins of a tower, a country turning

into the vast playing field
of another, a snow owl stretching

its almost-blue feathers—a point like a pause
in the unsettled dark.

II

Flight is panic or a source of attention—
I once thought—a tree shaking

its leaves in the midsummer storm, flight
is running or testing out tension—an absence

of words. In the story, the harbour carries
the moon like a warning—

the sea echoing traffic and light. Somewhere
someone is writing a letter, running

to send it on time. The night is precise like a knife
or a tape-measure, a highway

of lanterns—the night is an hour—an owl
circling a field of dark matter, the night

is a target—a moving
light chamber—a field ringing with lights.

III

In the dream a river cut through
a walled garden, a snow owl
was marking the time—every hour
the night turned into a chamber

of seconds, every hour a letter
hadn't arrived. The owl completed
a circle, the river turned into a line
in the dark, a glass chamber, a cut.

IV

You're a river, the dream
said—a fast river with wings, you're
a castle, the storm said, kind of new
and impossible to lift, you're a letter—
the road noted, a runner—the night
added, you're impatient, the snow owl
muttered, you're always waiting for words
to happen—you are something

I don't entirely get, the quick
winter declared—a river with snow owl
wings? You're a film of a river, the dream
said, not a real river, the boat
stressed, you're the heart of a castle, the rain
tried, you're a highway—the moon
said, but also a runner: you're a child
holding onto a letter, immature

and impatient—I think you're under
a lot of pressure, the letter
whispered from a faraway bridge,
you're the want of a letter, the river
said, you're the road going through
difficult weather, you're the runner somewhere
carrying a letter, a snow owl flapping
its dark river of wings

V

Imagine the street ringing with lanterns, the river raging
under a dark-silver mountain, the runner testing out knowledge
as if it were fractured by speed—take the making of stars

as lightest-glass chambers, the drawing of cities lying under
high fields, hold onto the sound driving towards the heart
of an incomplete bridge, hold the sea against sunset—nothing

matches this: somewhere someone is carrying a letter, trying out
absence as speed. The moon is a warning or a warm
invitation, the night is a rally—a field ringing with tears.

V I

You're a driver, the dream
said, it's a bit like a river but so much
faster, the night added, you're a telescope—
the moon tried, a strange one—the road
said—looking for words as faraway
stars, you're difficult weather, the highway
said, impatient—the owl hissed before
marking the night with a scar.

VII

In the picture I'm so well-behaved—
holding a letter like a symbol

of purpose. There is so much distance
but here's a thing, here's a game

of interpretation—
look at the picture, the girl holding the letter

like a play or an arrow carrying
stage directions—

here, she's not reading the letter only
to tear it apart a few seconds

later, or throw it into some improvised
fire—here she's holding it close, a gesture

of not falling apart. Oh, how I love
pictures—they tell you nothing and ask

for nothing—so much easier
than words. In the picture I'm so patient—

sitting forever on the pitch-perfect
rock. The moon is precise like a point

or a split second, the sea is intact. Flight is panic
or a source of attention—

you see, something
has happened—I don't think like this

anymore. The fields are moving—hold onto
the letter, let it take water and fire

for as long as it holds—I told you—memory
works best as geography—

somewhere someone is carrying a letter,
marking out distance with words.

VIII

You're a dreamer, the river
said, it's a bit like driving but so much
safer, the owl added, you're the highway
lying under a letter, a field stretching out
in the icy-blue weather, I think I've got it—the new
winter said—you're the runner
carrying a letter, running, yes—it's a bit like
grieving or being

impatient—the telescope
said, I'm not sure about that, the snow owl
muttered—it is more like flying or
testing out space, yes, that's what I meant—
the telescope said—it's all about
distance—a ship trying a lake, you're a dreamer—
the river said, it's a bit like driving but so much
scarier, the letter

stressed, you're the want
of a letter and the hold of a letter, a field
ringing with letters and letters, you're the runner
testing new information, you're a dreamer—
the river said, it's a bit like driving but with more
directions—running—the telescope
said—that's what it is, you're always moving, yes—you're
something I'm still trying to catch—

Absolute Scenes, The Banquet, The Citadel of the Mind, A Wandering
The quotes from Dante, in Italian and English translation, are taken from the following sources:

Dante, *Convivio, A Dual Language Critical Edition*, edited and trans. Andrew Frisardi (Cambridge University Press, 2018)

Dante, *The Divine Comedy*, trans. Robin Kirkpatrick (Penguin Classics, 2012)

Affogato
The first quote in the poem is taken from: "Lunch with the FT: Carlo Rovelli," *Financial Times*, August 12, 2016

The second quote is taken from: "Tom Stoppard's *Arcadia*, at Twenty," *The New Yorker*, August 8, 2013

Autumn
The poem is dedicated to Lior Bar—my childhood friend, my first friend, my heart.

Le Malheur a été Mon Dieu
The text in French is the complete opening section from Rimbaud's *Une Saison en Enfer*. In terms of form, I changed some of the original line breaks in order to create a dialogue with Rimbaud's words.

Love, an Accident in a Substance
The quotes in Italian and English are taken from: Dante, *Vita Nuova, A Dual Language Edition*, trans. Virginia Jewiss (Penguin Books, 2022)

Meaning Something is Like Going Towards Someone

The poem's title is taken from Wittgenstein, *Philosophical Investigations*, §457: *'Yes, meaning something is like going towards someone.'*

The Banquet

In addition to the quotes from Dante, other quotes are taken from the following sources:

Tom Stoppard, *Arcadia*, (Faber, 2009)

Wittgenstein, *Philosophical Investigations*, 4th ed., trans. G.E.M Anscombe, P.M.S. Hacker and Joachim Schulte (Blackwell Publishing, 2009)

ACKNOWLEDGEMENTS

Thank you to Michael Schmidt for your support and encouragement over the years, for creating this rarest of spaces in which words wander and breathe until they turn into poems. Thank you to John McAuliffe for your enthusiasm and thoughtfulness and invaluable editorial insight. Thank you both for making poetry happen.

Thank you to Kaddy Benyon, Lara Frankena, Lucy Hamilton, Megan Hunter, Lisa Kelly, and Lucy Sheerman, for your friendship and indispensable advice when reading my work.

My thanks to the editors of the magazines and publications in which the following poems first appeared:

"Absolute Scenes," "All Haulers," "Snow Leopard and Dark-Iris Lakes," "The Banquet," "The Citadel of the Mind," and "The Letter:" *PN Review*

"A Wandering:" *Poetry London*

"Meaning Something is like Going Towards Someone:" *Berlin Lit*

"Memory and Geography:" *The New Yorker*

"Self-Portrait as Autumn Fields:" *The Poetry Review*

"The Letter:" Highly Commended, *The Forward Book of Poetry 2024*

"The Pain or the Piano-Tuning:" *Poetry Ireland Review*

"Un Amour Désespéré:" *The Friday Poem*

*

"Film:" The poem featured in *Readings*: a collaboration between the Cambridge Poetry Festival and the Cambridge School of Art, Summer 2025.

"Affogato:" an early version of the poem was commissioned for *The Byron Festival at Trinity College*, Cambridge, 2024.

*

The Banquet was written with the support of the Authors' Foundation Grant. My thanks to The Society of Authors for providing me with much needed time and space towards the completion of this book.